gallery guide

GOYA

gallery guide

GOYA

Manuela B. Mena Marqués

Fundación Amigos del Museo del Prado

FLOOR PLAN OF THE PRADO MUSEUM

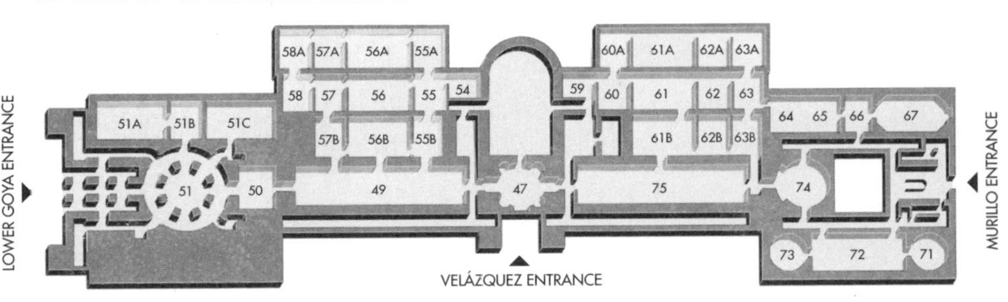
LOWER FLOOR
LOWER GOYA ENTRANCE
VELÁZQUEZ ENTRANCE
MURILLO ENTRANCE
58A 57A 56A 55A
58 57 56 55 54
57B 56B 55B
51A 51B 51C
51 50 49 47 75 74
59 60A 61A 62A 63A
60 61 62 63
61B 62B 63B
64 65 66 67
73 72 71

BASEMENT
102 101 100

Translation: María Luisa Balseiro, Everett Rice
Edition: Tf. Editores
Printed in Tf. Artes Gráficas, S. A., Alcobendas (Madrid)

ISBN: 978-84-95452-47-4
D.L: M-18711-2007

Cover: Goya, *The Countess of Chinchón* (detail),
Museo Nacional del Prado, Madrid

Third edition: March 2008

Due to the work being carried out in the Prado Museum, the exact location of the paintings described in this guide may vary. We regret any inconvenience which this set of circumstances may cause.

Introduction

The paintings of Francisco de Goya y Lucientes are among the most singular and defining values of the Prado, both in artistic and historical terms, and the sum of his paintings, drawings, and prints amounts to a monographic museum within the Museum itself. The nearly 150 works from his hand make it possible to study in depth, better here than anywhere else, one of the greatest artists of the Spanish school and indeed in world art. The Prado also houses 500 of his drawings and the series of his prints. The Museum's collection of Goya's paintings is valuable for the works themselves, but the interest of this collection also lies in the unique possibility it provides for studying his work in the context of Spanish painting in general, of Velázquez and Murillo, whom Goya deeply admired, and of the great European artists whose works he had known since his youth, Titian, Rubens, Tiepolo, and Mengs. Goya's painting connects easily with the tendencies of late eighteenth-century art and, consequently, with French Rococo or the late derivations of Italian Baroque art, such as the work of Corrado Giaquinto, and comparisons may be made with Goya's earlier style in order truly to understand what he owed to tradition and what was modern about his concept of painting.

The works which once decorated the walls of the *Quinta del Sordo*, the so-called "Black Paintings", bring the Prado's Goya collection to a close, along with the portrait of Muguiro, which may well have been the artist's last canvas. These works have given rise to an abundant literature, and with them the Prado Museum stands at the threshold of modernity. They are frightening and "black" in their meaning and they reveal the darkest and most sinister desires of mankind. Their strange and powerful beauty is far removed from the refined and exquisite tastes of the Rococo or the cold perfection of the canons of the Neoclassicism in which the artist had been trained. In Goya's hands Spanish art becomes one of the precursors of the modern world. Better than any written commentary or explanation, these works singlehandedly reveal the development of a mind that reached into the future, as geniuses characteristically do.

Chronologically, the rooms devoted to Goya in the Prado start with his tapestry cartoons. Except for a few isolated works that belong to other collections, the Museum owns virtually the whole series. These cartoons mark the starting point of his art and the beginning of his activity at the Spanish court. These large-scale canvases, which were painted to be used as models by the weavers at the newly-created Royal Tapestry Factory of Santa Bárbara, demonstrate Goya's gifts for composition, his sense of colour, the vigour of his painterly technique and his knowledge of classical painting and ancient sculpture, as well as the masterly ease with which he captures reality in a new and prodigious manner.

A superb series of portraits also enriches the Prado's Goya collection and allows the visitor to trace Goya's stylistic evolution in this difficult artistic genre, where success required the painter to combine the skill for producing a faithful likeness with a talent for covert flattery, representational inventiveness, and much less easy to define but nevertheless essential: the ability to capture the intimate individuality of his sitters.

The Prado is fortunate to own two examples of Goya's still-life painting. This genre had attained its greatest splendour in the seventeenth century, when the characteristics that define the Spanish *bodegón* were formulated, but Goya was to be one of its finest practitioners.

The Museum also includes some outstanding works in other subject areas such as "history painting", or scenes in which the artist narrates a story of some importance, though not always related to actual historical events. But consistent with classical tradition, in this kind of work Goya's art is always underpinned by his concern for men and their actions. In this sense, the most representative works are the two large canvases dealing with the Peninsular War.

The *capricho* or "caprice", a typically eighteenth-century genre, was endowed by Goya with unique qualities of absolute modernity and individuality. The Prado houses an exceptionally large and varied collection of such works which has been further enriched by recent acquisitions. The unique example from the series presented in 1793 to the Royal Academy of San Fernando, *The Strolling Players*, marks the beginning of his artistic independence, as the artist himself emphasized in his letters; but there are others, such as the small *Duchess of Alba and "La Beata"*, or the *Flying Witches*, that bear witness to the creative freedom that was foreshadowed in cartoon sketches such as *The Meadow of San Isidro*. Besides the works already mentioned, any visit to the Prado's Goya collection must of course include the extraordinary *Majas*, one of them naked, the other fully clothed.

Dining Room of the Prince and Princess of Asturias, El Escorial, 1775

In 1775, while still working under the direction of his brother-in-law Bayeu, Goya secured his first commission as a painter of tapestry cartoons to decorate the dining room of the prince and princess at El Escorial. There Goya would strike a new departure from the traditional iconography of great hunts, depicting everyday scenes in a realistic style.

Dogs in Leash (Cat. 753)

Oil on canvas, 112 x 174 cm

Hunt with Decoy (Cat. 2856)

Oil on canvas, 112 x 176 cm

Hunting Party (Cat. 2857)

Oil on canvas, 290 x 226 cm

Hunter Loading his Rifle (Cat. 5539)

Oil on canvas, 289 x 90 cm

Hunter with his Dogs (Cat. 805)

Oil on canvas, 262 x 71 cm

The Angler (Cat. 5542)

Oil on canvas, 289 x 110 cm

Dining Room of the Prince and Princess of Asturias, Palace of El Pardo, 1776-1778

The palace of El Pardo, set in a magnificent park near Madrid that had been a royal hunting ground from early times, was again put to use by the Bourbon kings as a leisure retreat, especially since the accession of the nature-loving Charles III, and became one of their favourite residences. The decorating of this palace that combined with the enlightened tastes of the time and the desire of monarchs to enter into closer terms with their subjects, may explain the choice of subject matter from daily life and popular amusements: the portrayal of Madrid *majos* and *majas*, or smart young men and women from the lower classes, is an absolute novelty.

The Picnic (Cat. 768)
Oil on canvas, 271 x 295 cm

A group of *majos* on the bank of the Manzanares River, with the hermitage of the Virgen del Puerto clearly identifiable on the right.

Dance on the Bank of the Manzanares River (Cat. 769)
Oil on canvas, 272 x 295 cm

The rhythm of the counter-poised couples getting ready for the dance makes for a scene of great beauty. The dance shown is the popular *seguidilla,* less lively than the famous *fandango.*

Fight at the New Inn (Cat. 770)
Oil on canvas, 275 x 414 cm

Describing this composition in his invoice, Goya supplied some noteworthy particulars, e. g. the fact that the men gathering at the *venta,* or roadside inn, are "coachmen and muleteers from several provinces of Spain", recognizable by their garb, such as "the man from Murcia" with his back turned in the foreground. The brawl started over a game of cards, and everyone has more or less violently entered the fray.

A Promenade in Andalusia (Cat. 771)
Oil on canvas, 275 x 190 cm

This is a direct forerunner of some of the most characteristic etchings in the *Caprichos* series, dealing with the intrigues of love and jealousy.

The Parasol (Cat. 773)
Oil on canvas, 104 x 152 cm

This is one of the loveliest examples of Goya's early painting. His acquaintance with the Old Masters is applied unobtrusively.

Boys Inflating a Bladder (Cat. 776)
Oil on canvas, 116 x 124
Boys Picking Fruit (Cat. 777)
Oil on canvas, 119 x 122 cm

These are among Goya's earliest portrayals of childhood, but they already show his full grasp of the candor and liveliness of children's games.

Antechamber to the Bedroom of the Prince and Princess of Asturias, Palace of El Pardo, 1778

In October 1777, as Goya was completing the cartoons for the dining room of the prince and princess in El Pardo, he was ordered to go on with sets for their sleeping quarters in that palace. Some of the resulting pieces are among the best-known in his oeuvre, e. g. *The Crockery Vendor, The Amateur Bullfight* or *Boys Playing Soldiers.* This set of cartoons centres on different facets of life in Madrid.

The Blind Guitarist (Cat. 778)
Oil on canvas, 260 x 311 cm

Goya described it in minute detail, referring to the fashionable gentleman as "a foreigner" and mentioning the black waterseller and a baker: this is the world of those "street cries" that were first portrayed by artists in late sixteenth-century Italy.

The Crockery Vendor (Cat. 780)
Oil on canvas, 259 x 220 cm

One of the most elaborate compositions in the series, Goya setting the static but emotionally conflicting foreground, with the young girls, the old woman and the vendor, against the swift movement of the coach carrying the lady. As in the best pieces by Watteau, figures seen from the back play an equally important and suggestive role as those in frontal view; their opposition, a device which goes back to Italian Renaissance painting, is here used to diversify and balance the groups, as well as to enhance the timeless beauty of an everyday scene that is nevertheless sensed as charged with meaning.

Boys Playing Soldiers (Cat. 783)
Oil on canvas, 146 x 94 cm

The vigour and liveliness of the chief little soldier, his martial bearing, and the amusing, childish pride with which he faces the viewer mark this as one of the highest achievements in the portrayal of children to be found in the whole of Goya's oeuvre.

The Ball Game (Cat. 784)
Oil on canvas, 261 x 470 cm

Goya worked out this large composition to replace *The Blind Guitarist* as the centrepiece in the bedroom decoration.

The Swing (Cat. 785)
Oil on canvas, 260 x 165 cm

The swing was frequently depicted in eighteenth-century painting, often, as in Boucher and Fragonard, with little-disguised erotic overtones. Goya here introduces it in what appears to be a peaceable family scene.

The Washerwomen (Cat. 786)
Oil on canvas, 218 x 166 cm

The landscape in this work is one of the most naturalistic and beautiful in the whole series.

The Amateur Bullfight (Cat. 787)
Oil on canvas, 259 x 136 cm

It has been suggested that the young bullfighter's features are those of Goya himself, who was a great fan of bullfighting.

The Tobacco Guard (Cat. 788)
Oil on canvas, 262 x 137 cm

Tobacco was a state monopoly in the eighteenth century, and since it was highly priced it was object of smugglers. Fetched high prices, and that illegal trade was a subject of topical interest and criticism in popular literature, where the law and its keepers are not rated for their efficiency.

The Woodcutters (Cat. 791)
Oil on canvas, 141 x 114 cm
The Majo with a Guitar (Cat. 743)
Oil on canvas, 137 x 112 cm
The Rendezvous (Cat. 792)
Oil on canvas, 100 x 151 cm

These cartoons evince a summary, shorthand technique, with energetic brushwork boldly and swiftly applied to the reddish underpainting with no attempt to cover it up.

Cat. 791

Private Dining Room of the Prince of Asturias, Palace of El Pardo, 1786-1788

After a six-year interval, the Royal Tapestry Factory commissioned a new series from Goya, this time to furnish the private dining room of the Prince of Asturias in the Palace of El Pardo. The cartoons were completed in the following year and the tapestries were woven; however, due of the death of Charles III, they were never installed in their original destination, but rather were used at random to decorate different rooms in the royal apartments at El Escorial. The theme chosen by Goya for the prince´s private apartments was one that had a long iconographic tradition, the Four Seasons.

The Flower Girls (Spring) (Cat. 793)
Oil on canvas, 277 x 192 cm

A particularly lovely scene, pivoting on the elegance of the young woman who kneels in the foreground, in an echo of Velázquez's *Las Meninas.* She is offering a rose to the woman in the center, who is herself loaded with roses.

The Threshing Floor (Summer) (Cat. 794)
Oil on canvas, 276 x 641 cm

Goya has made here a lavish display of sheaves of wheat, the prime emblem of the goddess Ceres, who traditionally personified summer and the harvest in European painting. Country life is represented by the harvesters resting in the heat of summer: they are joined by their happy and smiling families in teasing a poor wretch whom they would like to get dead drunk.

The Grape Harvest (Autumn) (Cat. 795)
Oil on canvas, 275 x 190 cm

The traditional iconography of the grape harvest is used here as an allegory of autumn. The airy, glowing landscape in which the gatherers are working reflects the tranquillity of the country-side and of nature as a whole. The smartly-dressed lady pensively reaches for the bunch of grapes proffered by a hand-some *majo* attired in yellow, the colour of autumn, while the little boy, dressed up like a tiny prince, tries in vain to get his share of the savoury grapes, seemingly reserved for the grown-ups.

The Snowstorm (Winter) (Cat. 798)
Oil on canvas, 275 x 293 cm

Winter is here signified by the blizzard and the snow-covered fields. Three peasants, wrapped in their blankets, return from an apparently unsuccessful trip to purchase a pig, since they proceed empty-handed, their dismal looks betraying cold and hunger. Two other men have had better luck: one covers himself with a hat and a warm cape, the other is dressed in livery, which possibly means that they are the servants of some nobleman. They are leading a mule, rather ornately harnessed and loaded with a huge pork cut down the middle.

The Wounded Mason (Cat. 796)
Oil on canvas, 268 x 110 cm

This is one of the most famous among Goya's tapestry cartoons, and it has been cited as proof of his concern for social issues, since it apparently shows a bricklayer injured on the job.

Poor People at a Fountain
(Cat. 797)
Oil on canvas, 277 x 115 cm

The young mother, finely dressed with a shawl, red stockings and silver buckles on her black shoes, gazes tenderly and forbearingly at her youngest son while he bawls in a rage, perhaps because he has not been allowed to carry one of the jugs like his older brother.

Two Cats Fighting (Cat. 6323)
Oil on canvas, 56 x 193 cm

A Magpie on a Tree Branch (Cat. 7346)
Oil on canvas, 279 x 28 cm

These are cartoons for tapestries intended to hang over a doorway and in a corner, respectively. The cats pick up a frequent theme in Goya's oeuvre.

Bedroom of the Infantas, Palace of El Pardo, 1788-1789

In 1788 Goya was given a new commission, which he only completed in part: the cartoons for tapestries to decorate the bedroom of the Infantas, the daughters of the Prince and Princess of Asturias. The death of King Charles III at the end of that year meant the abandonment of El Pardo, for the new royal pair preferred the palaces of La Granja, Aranjuez and El Escorial. The project is known from sketches preserved in the Museum.

Blindman's Bluff (Cat. 804)
Oil on canvas, 269 x 350 cm

Young persons dressed as *majos* and *majas* predominate in the merry circle, males alternating with females.

It seems clear that the *majo* wielding a ladle in the center must have for his partner the young woman who in the preliminary sketch (Cat. 2781) is seen hiding behind the lady, apart from the ring. For some reason, Goya erased her out of the picture after having put her in.

The King's Office, El Escorial, 1791-1792

In April 1790 Goya was commissioned to furnish the cartoons for tapestries to be hung in the newly-crowned Charles IV's office within the royal apartments in the monastery of El Escorial. But at the end of 1792 he was taken with the illness that would leave him deaf, and after his recovery he did not go on with the commission. Charles IV had desired for his office "rustic and jolly subjects".

The Wedding (Cat. 799)
Oil on canvas, 269 x 396 cm

This must count as one of the "jolly subjects" demanded by the king, although it reflects some of the deepest concerns of Goya the enlightened thinker. The lovely young woman in the centre, rather elaborately dressed up, has just been married to an obese, ugly man, obviously rich, whose profile resembles a pig's snout.

Girls with Water Jugs (Cat. 800)
Oil on canvas, 262 x 160 cm

Both the girl in the foreground and the elder woman stare at the viewer with a knowing smile of complicity, as does their young escort; but only the girls precariously balance on their heads the water jugs, a traditional symbol of female virtue.

The Straw Mannekin (Cat. 802)
Oil on canvas, 267 x 160 cm

The game of tossing a dummy in a blanket, a Carnival entertainment by its use of masks and mockery, becomes a clear Goyesque allegory of women's dominance over men.

The Little Giants (Cats. 7112)
Oil on canvas, 137 x 104 cm
Boys Climbing a Tree (Cats. 803)
Oil on canvas, and 141 x 111 cm

In *The Little Giants* the boys seem to mimic the game of the adult stiltwalkers, except that they ride piggyback on their playmates' shoulders.

Sketches for Tapestry Cartoons

The Prado Museum has five of the most beautiful preparatory sketches for the tapestry cartoons of the Royal Tapestry Factory of Santa Bárbara. The *Fight at the Cock Inn* entered the Museum in 2002. The other four, *The Drunken Mason*, *Blindman's Bluff*, *The Hermitage of San Isidro on his Feast Day*, and *The Meadow of San Isidro* were purchased in 1798 by the Duke and Duchess of Osuna, to be hung in *La Alameda*, their pleasure villa on the outskirts of Madrid which already housed other works by Goya.

Fight at the Cock Inn (Cat. 7801)

Oil on canvas, 42 x 67.3 cm

Preparatory sketch for the tapestry cartoon called *Fight at the New Inn.* It is the only preparatory work that has survived from those made for the first series of tapestries.

These cartoons met with immediate success, due to the beauty of their technique and colour. They were immediately appreciated by contemporary collectors as independent cabinet pictures.

The Drunken Mason (Cat. 2782)
Oil on canvas, 35 x 15 cm

A model for the cartoon *The Wounded Mason* (Cat. 796). The modern title may be misleading, since, just as in the larger version, the man carried by his fellow workers is hurt: blood trickles from his left temple and down his shirt. The amused expression on his workmates' faces surely relates to the fact that he is in shirt-sleeves, with no trousers and one of his stockings hanging down, which makes the traditional interpretation of the cartoon as a sort of social commentary rather unlikely.

Blindman's Bluff (Cat. 2781)
Oil on canvas, 41 x 44 cm

The epitomy of the lowbrow charm of Madrilenian *majos* and *majas,* a far cry from the idealized world of French rococo art. The three sketches for the cartoons of tapestries to decorate the Infantas' bedroom in the Pardo Palace are without any doubt among the most significant and popular of Goya's works in the Prado.

The Hermitage of San Isidro on his Feast Day (Cat. 2783)
Oil on canvas, 42 x 44 cm

This sketch shows the hermitage of Madrid's patron saint on his feast day, the 15th of May. Young women dressed as *majas* are sitting on the ground in front of the chapel, waiting for their *majos* to bring them water to drink from the miraculous spring where a crowd lines up in the background. The theme is related to that of *The Meadow of San Isidro.*

The Meadow of San Isidro (Cat. 750)
Oil on canvas, 42 x 90 cm

The best-known piece in the series and also the most significant. Goya mentioned *The Meadow* in his letters to Martín Zapater, his childhood friend in Saragossa, telling him of the difficulty of the task, with so many diverse groups of figures to cram into a small canvas. The composition is very precise, fully suggestive of the bustling festivity of the crowd sitting on the bank of the Manzanares River. The landscape opens up toward the river; beyond extends a topographically exact panorama of Madrid, where the bulky Royal Palace and Seminary are clearly visible, as well as the large dome of San Francisco el Grande and several easily recognized spires.

Strolling Players (Cat. 3045)
Oil on canvas, 43 x 32 cm

This picture, painted on tin, was part of a set of twelve scenes of bullfights and sundry subjects that the artist presented to the Academy of San Fernando in January 1794, after his serious illness the year before, which left him deaf. The handling is precise and very brilliant, with small and varied brush strokes, full of rhythm and movement, that stand out on the tin surface. On a makeshift stage above the sign "ALEC MEN", meaning "Alegoría Menandrea", a satirical comedy is being played, in the style of those by the Greek Menander, a genre connected also with the Italian *Commedia dell'Arte.*

The Duchess of Alba and "La Beata" (Cat. 7020)
Oil on canvas, 30 x 25 cm

The light-hearted, girlish character of the duchess is reflected in this small canvas signed "Goya Año 1795". Cayetana, in a yellow dress, with her back turned but identifiable by her lavish head of dark curly hair, is shown playing a prank on her duenna Rafaela Luisa Velázquez, nicknamed "La Beata".

A Picador on Horseback (Cat. 744)
Oil on canvas, 57 x 47 cm

This was one of the pictures transferred from the Royal Palace to make up the initial core of the Prado collection, listed in its first catalogue (1821) as "Un picador a caballo". The very "Goyesque" motif of a mounted bullfighter guarded the picture's secret until recent X-ray studies revealed an underlying equestrian portrait of Manuel Godoy.

Flying Witches (Cat. 7748)
Oil on canvas, 43 x 30 cm

This is one of a set of six small canvases with sorcery scenes that the Duke and Duchess of Osuna purchased from

Goya in 1798, for their suburban villa near Madrid, *La Alameda*. Sorcery was a fashionable topic among aristocrats in the late eighteenth century; for the enlightened circles that Goya frequented, however, belief in witches was one of the evils of ignorance, a vulgar fraud, inimical to progress and reason.

The Naked Maja (Cat. 742)
Oil on canvas, 97 x 190 cm

This image, whose riddle has yet to be solved, is an exercise in confidential painting, a development of the cabinet picture tradition, and the "capricho" *par excellence* in its depiction, at once traditional and new, of the reclining female nude. This is no longer a classical Venus, perfect of body and face, escorted by Cupid; on the contrary, she is a living woman not exempt from blemishes, in spite of the undeniable allure and loveliness of her naked body. The painting was first recorded by Agustín Ceán Bermúdez and the engraver Pedro González de Sepúlveda, who in 1800 described it, fully installed and alone, without its clothed counterpart, in a private cabinet of Manuel Godoy's palace, along with other female nudes of classical stock, namely

Velázquez's *Venus and Cupid* and a sixteenth-century Italian Venus, both of them gifts from the Duchess of Alba to Godoy, and a copy of a Venus by Titian. Pictures of female nudity had been banned in Spain in the closing years of the eighteenth century, and both Charles III and Charles IV had considered destroying some works of that character in the royal collection; but apparently Godoy was accorded the exceptional privilege of keeping this kind of painting, albeit in the privacy of his rooms.

A rumour starting very early in the nineteenth century had it that the model was the Duchess of Alba, painted at the time of her affair with the artist in her estate of Sanlúcar de Barrameda, in 1796-1797. Others have suggested that she was Godoy's mistress Pepita Tudó, on the assumption that it was the queen's favourite who commissioned the work; in that case there would have been a still stronger reason to conceal the model's true face. By its outstanding expressive force, this painting has become a symbol of womanhood.

The Clothed Maja (Cat. 741)
Oil on canvas, 95 x 190 cm

The Clothed Maja is first documented in an inventory made in 1808 by the French painter Frédéric Quilliet, José Bonaparte's agent, who lists it along with *The Naked Maja.* Both were mentioned again in 1813, as "Gitanas", gypsies, in the inventory made when Ferdinand VII seized the property of Godoy, and two years later they crop up in a report of the Secret Chamber of the Inquisition dated March 16, 1815, where one reads that "this Court hereby summons the aforesaid Goya to appear before it, to identify and declare whether they are his work, his motive for making them, commissioned by whom, and to what end". Once again, nothing is known about its commission, but the fact that it was not mentioned with its nude equivalent in 1800 might mean that it was done later, perhaps to dissimulate or cover the first.

Commerce (Cat. 2546)
Agriculture (Cat. 2547)
Industry (Cat. 2548)
Tempera on canvas, 227 cm Ø, each one

Cat. 2546

In late 1804 work was completed on the remodelling of Godoy's official residence in Madrid, which comprised building a vast hall of entrance and a grand staircase. Shortly afterwards, that magnificent entry was fitted with huge tondos that the prime minister had commissioned from Goya, to be painted in tempera with allegorical subjects. The allegories chosen were meant to portray the ideological foundations of wealth and progress in a new, enlightened Spain: Science (now lost), Agriculture, Industry and Commerce.

Agriculture is represented, following an iconographical tradition, by the figure of the classical goddess Ceres. *Commerce* is signified by merchants from the Levant. For *Industry* Goya envisioned an allegory based on weaving that calls to mind Velázquez's renowned *Spinners,* with two women at the spinning-wheel.

Dead Turkey (Cat. 751)
Oil on canvas, 45 x 62 cm
Dead Fowl (Cat. 752)
Oil on canvas, 46 x 62 cm

Cat. 752

These are two of a set of twelve still lifes belonging to Goya himself that were listed in an inventory of his property drawn up when his wife, Josefa Bayeu, died in 1812. He painted them as a decoration for his own home, surrounding himself with images that must have reminded him of his hunting feats. The sombre mood conveyed by the artist's insistence on the realistic rendering of dead animals has been taken as a sign that they were painted during the tragic years of the Peninsular War.

The technical virtuosity of these two still lifes (the second signed "Goya") flawlessly reflects the distinctive quality of feathers as widely different as those of turkeys and hens.

The Second of May 1808 in Madrid: The Fight against the Mamelukes (Cat. 748)

Oil on canvas, 268 x 347 cm

The patriotism of Goya, who took up a resolute stance against the French invaders during the War of Independence, urged him to pay a tribute to the heroes of that struggle. Thus, when economic hardship struck him in the years following, he approached the regent, cardinal Luis de Borbón, with a proposal to celebrate some actions of the war in painting. His true feelings show through the catchphrases of rhetoric: "... to perpetuate by means of the brush the most notable and

heroic actions and scenes of our glorious insurrection against the tyrant of Europe". He was granted a monthly stipend of 1.500 *reales* to execute four paintings, only two of which were completed. Their destination has never been precisely ascertained; it may have been a public monument to the Madrid heroes. Goya chose to illustrate two highly significant episodes, since it was the revolt of Madrilenians on May 2, 1808, that marked the beginning of the war, and the subsequent repression, with the shooting of prisoners, many of them innocent, reflected the cruelty of the war, the violence unleashed by the invasion, and the sufferings of the people, reduced to the role of a guiltless victim of events.

The scene of the Second of May shows the fierce, outraged onslaught of the commoners who, armed with knives and poniards, as true accounts testify, desperately attacked the mamelukes in the streets of Madrid, trying to prevent the departure of members of the royal family.

The Third of May 1808 in Madrid: The Executions on Príncipe Pío Hill (Cat. 749)
Oil on canvas, 268 x 347 cm

The tragic events that followed on the people's uprising in Madrid on May 2, 1808, were well known to Spaniards. Literary descriptions and popular prints reported the French army's cruel repression of the people. Anyone the invaders caught bearing a knife – as craftsmen in Madrid usually did – was to be shot; and, according to Toreno, "they

continued into the next morning, shooting some who had been arrested the day before, and they chose for the executions the fenced-in field of the house of Príncipe Pío", in the Moncloa neighbourhood. The cheap prints minutely described the firing squads and their victims, but Goya has painted a scene that transcends the actual event to become a symbol of the innocence of victims, whose protagonism is absolute.

The night setting emphasizes the drama of the action, and the glare of the soldiers' lamp is focused on those who are about to die, some of them terrified at their inescapable fate, others furious but powerless. It also illuminates those who have already died, heaped in a bloody pile in the foreground; approaching from the dark distance may be seen some compassionate women, who combine with other details to confer on the scene the holy status of a sacrifice of innocents.

The Colossus (Cat. 2785)
Oil on canvas, 116 x 105 cm

This painting has traditionally been identified with the one listed as "Un gigante", a giant, in the inventory of Goya's possessions drawn up in 1812, after the death of his wife. X-rays have revealed a totally different composition underneath, a blank, apparently unfinished landscape with the giant facing the viewer, his figure based on the Farnese Hercules, a classical sculpture that Goya copied more than once in his Italian Sketchbook.

The Milkmaid of Bordeaux (Cat. 2899)
Oil on canvas, 74 x 68 cm

This minor painting was inordinately praised by early twentieth-century Spanish critics who were eager to establish it as a necessary precedent of Impressionism.

The Holy Family with Saint John the Baptist as a Child

(Cat. 746), oil on canvas, 203 x 143 cm

No clue remains as to the original destination of this curious and lovely painting, which depicts one of the subjects most often repeated in Western art.

The woman's features, her face a perfect classical oval, her lips brightly red and full, her dark flowing hair framing her countenance, are still reminiscent of those of the Virgin and her female companions in the paintings of the Charterhouse of Aula Dei in Saragossa, painted by Goya in 1774.

The Immaculate Conception (Cat. 3260)

Oil on canvas, 80 x 41 cm

A preliminary study for the main altarpiece, lost in the Peninsular War, of the church of the College of Calatrava in Salamanca, a work recorded in 1783-1784 as a commission of Gaspar Melchor de Jovellanos, president of the Order of Calatrava, to whom this sketch belonged.

Christ on the Cross (Cat. 745)
Oil on canvas, 255 x 154 cm

With this painting, presented to the Royal Academy of Fine Arts of San Fernando in May 1780, Goya was finally admitted into that noble and progressive institution as an academician of merit, a status to which he had repeatedly aspired. The figure of Christ, lit up against a very dark background, bears deeply devout echoes of seventeenth-century Spanish painting.

The Holy Family (Cat. 7857)
Oil on canvas, 64 x 52 cm
Tobias and the Archangel Raphael (Cat. 7856)
Oil on canvas, 64 x 52 cm

These two pictures form a pair and are an example of painting made for private devotional purposes. Dated around 1787, in technique and in their human models they are closely related to *The Meadow of San Isidro* and the altar paintings for

the Convent of Santa Ana at Valladolid. From an iconographical point of view, both compositions are interrelated since the subject of Tobias and the Archangel Raphael was a Biblical precedent for The Virgin Mary with the Christ Child and Saint Joseph. Light plays a principal role in both works and reveals Goya's capacity for observation and analysis, as well as his mastery in capturing reality on canvas.

The Arrest of Christ (Cat. 3113)
Oil on canvas, 40 x 23 cm

A sketch for an altarpiece in the sacristy of Toledo Cathedral, and one of the most interesting works by Goya because of its intrinsic and startlingly modern beauty, its swift, energetic and abstract brushwork defining the whole and the details with strict accuracy.

Saint John the Baptist as a Boy in the Wilderness (Cat. 7853)
Oil on canvas, 112 x 81.5 cm.

On the back there is an inscription "X 20" which identifies this work with the canvas that appears in the inventory of the assets of Goya and his wife which was made after her death in 1812. It was sold in Paris in 1868 and its whereabouts were unknown until 2001. Goya has depicted a subject which is traditional in Italian and

Spanish painting, but he has treated it in a fresh and personal manner. The strong adolescent figure is filled with fervour and it reveals Goya's commitment to his art. The artist undoubtedly studied earlier compositions and religious texts in order to reflect the brave and difficult figure of Saint John the Baptist with veracity and realism.

Saints Justa and Rufina (Cat. 2650)
Oil on canvas, 47 x 29 cm

A friend of Goya, the scholar and collector Ceán Bermúdez, asked him for a painting on this subject to hang in the sacristy of Seville Cathedral. This sketch on panel is the single remaining preliminary study, and it may have been also the last one, since it hardly differs from the final work. Goya travelled to Seville to examine the intented location and acquaint himself with other images of the city's patron saints. He kept to the traditional iconography of the two young martyrs, who are shown holding the palms of martyrdom and the clay vessels of their potter's trade; he also deferred to the local belief that they had protected the city during the earthquake of 1504 and so placed in the background the Cathedral and the Giralda tower, which, according to the pious Sevillian legend, the two saints had miraculously held up.

King Charles IV in Court Costume (Cat. 3224)
Oil on canvas, 203 x 137 cm
Queen María Luisa in a Farthingale (Cat. 2862)
Oil on canvas, 220 x 140 cm

In January 1789 Goya was commissioned to paint the first official portraits of the new monarchs after Charles III's demise. Both are portrayed full-length on large-format canvases, in court dress and wearing the insignia of royalty.

Equestrian Portrait of King Charles IV (Cat. 719)
Oil on canvas, 336 x 282 cm
Equestrian Portrait of Queen María Luisa (Cat. 720)
Oil on canvas, 338 x 282 cm

Along with *The Family of Charles IV* and *A Picador on Horseback,* these portraits were the only specimens of Goya's art that hung in the Prado Museum when it first opened in 1819, while the painter was still alive. Dated first is that of the queen, riding on *Marcial,*

a gift from Godoy. Goya modelled his equestrian portraits on those painted by Velázquez for the Hall of Realms in the Buen Retiro Palace (now in the Prado), which he knew well, having made etched copies of them some years back.

The Family of Charles IV (Cat. 726)
Oil on canvas, 280 x 336 cm

The grand family portrait of Charles IV is one of the main pillars of Goya's oeuvre and a sure guide to his style. It was painted in Aranjuez and Madrid during the spring and summer of 1800. There was a clear precedent in Spain for this kind of group portrait of royalty, a canvas where the French painter Van Loo had presented the family of

Philip V, grandfather of Charles IV (Prado Museum, Cat. 2283). The fact that Goya may be seen at his easel on the left, like Velázquez in *Las Meninas,* has prompted critics to stress unfailingly his indebtedness to that famous work, even though that is the only parallel to be found between both paintings, which in terms of subject, technique or composition are other-wise totally unrelated. Goya's picture is profoundly original, and his robust rendering stands as a symbol of the Bourbon monarchy and the protagonists of an era that came to an abrupt end with the invasion of Spain by Napoleon's troops and the War of Independence.

The centre of the stage is held by the frontal figure of the queen, her head turned slightly to the right with the smiling, attractive expression she wears in all her portraits. She is embracing her youngest daughter, the Infanta María Isabel, and holding the hand of her youngest son, the Infante Francisco de Paula, who links her figure to that of the king. Charles is standing somewhat apart and nearer the picture plane, like his eldest son, who appears on the left, dressed in blue. By that means Goya symbolically sets off young Ferdinand as the Prince of Asturias and heir to the throne, placing behind him the Infante Carlos María Isidro, second in the line of succession. Next to the Prince may be seen the aged face of the king's sister, the Infanta María Josefa, and an unidentified young woman. Standing on the right behind the king is his brother, the Infante Antonio Pascual, and, seen in profile, the queen of Portugal Carlota Joaquina, no longer in Spain at the time. Closing the composition on the right stand the prince and princess of Parma, María Luisa Josefina and Luis de Borbón, who later became king of Etruria; the princess holds in her arms their son, the Infante Carlos Luis.

Sketches for *The Family of Charles IV*

María Josefa (Cat. 729)
Francisco de Paula (Cat. 730)
Antonio Pascual (Cat. 733)
Oil on canvas, 72 x 59 cm, each one
Carlos María Isidro (Cat. 731)
Luis (Cat. 732)
Oil on canvas, 74 x 60 cm, each one

The Prado Museum owns five of the ten preliminary sketches that are recorded for *The Family of Charles IV,* executed by the painter in Aranjuez in June and July 1800. They share a more or less uniform size and an orange-reddish underpainting on which Goya summarily and quickly noted down the features of several of the king's relatives in half-length.

King Ferdinand VII in a Royal Mantle (Cat. 735)
Oil on canvas, 206 x 143 cm

Ferdinand VII was born in El Escorial in 1784, the first son of Charles IV and María Luisa, and ascended the throne in 1808. In 1815, when he had abolished the Constitution and was reigning as an absolute monarch, he ruthlessly repressed any liberal move. The young king is here shown with the insignia of royalty, in a crimson mantle lined with ermine and holding the scepter with the arms of Castile and León; he wears the sash of Charles III and the collar of the Golden Fleece. Some pentimenti suggest that Goya elaborated his image directly in front of the model; hence the astonishing mastery of the expression, with the vacuous smile belied by a suspicious glance.

María Teresa de Vallabriga y Rozas (Cat. 7695)
Oil on canvas, 48 x 40 cm

María Teresa de Vallabriga, the daughter of minor nobles in Aragón, was married in 1776 to Luis de Borbón, brother of Charles III, who thereupon forfeited his and his descendants' rights to the throne. María Teresa, who was born in 1759, is seen here a few years after her marriage. The wooden base produces an enamel-like surface, while the dark, almost black underpainting highlights the terse and glowing whiteness of the youthful face.

The Family of the Duke and Duchess of Osuna (Cat. 739)
Oil on canvas, 225 x 171 cm

An exceptional instance of family portraiture in Spanish painting, this canvas shows the aristocrats Josefa Alonso de Pimentel, countess-duchess of Benavente, and Pedro Téllez Girón, the ninth duke of Osuna, who were among the earliest and most steadfast of Goya's patrons. They are accompanied by their children at that time: Josefa Manuela, the eldest, standing beside her father; Joaquina, later marchioness of Santa Cruz (Cat. 7070); Francisco de Borja, the future duke of Osuna, playfully riding on a stick; and in the foreground, sitting on a cushion and holding the string of a toy carriage, the youngest son, Pedro de Alcántara, later prince of Anglona and future director of the Prado Museum during the liberal triennium, from 1821 to 1823. The duke, dressed in uniform, was a soldier by training, a leading figure of the Enlightenment and a man of varied cultural and scientific interests. He presided over the Economic Society of Madrid and was a member of the Royal Spanish Academy. The duchess, who patronized writers and artists and presided over the ladies' board of the Economic Society of Madrid, wears a dress in the French fashion, with rare and costly hand-painted buttons. The children are attired in the kind of comfortable and loose-fitting clothes that the ideas of the Enlightenment prescribed for them.

María Antonia Gonzaga, Dowager Marchioness of Villafranca (Cat. 2447)
Oil on canvas, 87 x 72 cm

Widowed in 1773 of Antonio Álvarez de Toledo, the tenth marquis of Villafranca, she was the mother of don José Álvarez de Toledo, the eleventh marquis of Villafranca, and duke of Alba by his marriage. This intimate image, exempt of the formalities and elaborate pomp of full-length portraits, shows her dressed with elegance and some coquetry; she is holding a closed fan, and her attitude would seem to denote calm patience and authority.

The Marquis of Villafranca (Cat. 2449)
Oil on canvas, 195 x 126 cm

José Álvarez de Toledo y Gonzaga, born the eldest son in 1756, inherited the family title of marquis of Villafranca on the death of his father in 1773. He married Cayetana, Duchess of Alba, in 1775, when he was nineteen and she thirteen, but died childless in 1796. He was a man of artistic and musical tastes, and a counsellor of the Royal Academy; he reputedly played the violin like a virtuoso, he collected musical instruments, and he commissioned works directly from Haydn.

He is portrayed leaning on his elbow on a pianoforte and gazing at the viewer as if to comment on the score, inscribed "Four Songs with Pianoforte Accompaniment, by Mr. Haydn". By his delicate features and hands and his refined pose, Goya conveys the sensitivity of the aristocrat and his love of music; but by presenting him in a smart riding habit complete with boots and spurs, his hat just put down on the piano, he is also suggesting, with his characteristic shrewdness, that the marquis wanted to have emphasized the virile interests that befit a nobleman.

The Painter Francisco Bayeu y Subías (Cat. 721)
Oil on canvas, 112 x 84 cm

Bayeu was royal painter, director of the Academy of San Fernando and one of the leading figures in late eighteenth-century Spanish art. His portrait was commissioned from Goya by his daughter Feliciana Bayeu as a gift to the Academy in August 1795, upon the elder painter's death. It was delivered unfinished.

Self-Portrait (Cat. 7775)
Oil on canvas, 18 x 12 cm

This small self-portrait belonged to the duchess of Alba, who bequeathed it to her butler Tomás de Berganza. It must have been a gift from the artist to that celebrated aristocrat at the time of their closest association, in 1795-1797, when Goya became intimate with Cayetana to the point of being her guest for some months at her estate in Sanlúcar de Barrameda.

Gaspar Melchor de Jovellanos (Cat. 3236)
Oil on canvas, 204 x 113 cm

This portrait, signed "JOVELLANOS/POR/GOYA", is dated in 1798, when the sitter was Minister of Justice. A prominent bronze statue of the goddess Minerva, set on a solid pedestal behind the politician's desk, seems to extend towards him a protecting hand, while leaning on a shield with the arms of the Royal Asturian Institute of Navigation and Mineralogy, which Jovellanos had founded.

An Asturian by birth, interested in the arts and sciences, Gaspar Melchor de Jovellanos played a leading role in the cultural and political life of Spain during the last third of

the eighteenth century. His enlightened ideas are well known through his abundant and manifold writings on social and political issues, and from his position as a minister he tried to bring about significant reforms. Here he appears sitting on a carved and gilt armchair before a magnificent matching desk.

Goya has succeeded in capturing his serene, intelligent gaze; while placing him in a sumptuous setting, he shows him dressed with sober elegance, in an ermine-lined dress coat surprisingly devoid of the decorations, that were a usual adjunct of the images of public men.

General José de Urrutia (Cat. 736)

Oil on canvas, 199 x 133 cm

Urrutia, born in 1739 in the Biscayan district of Zalla and deceased in 1809, attained to the honourable rank of captain-general by his own merits and valour on the battlefield. In 1789 he fought in the first Crimean war, and his conduct at the siege of Ozaku earned him the Cross of Saint George from the empress Catherine of Russia, who sent it along with a golden sword. In 1794 he was appointed captain-general of Catalonia, and confirmed the following year, after the Peace of Basel; but some time later he was discharged from all public duties owing to differences with Godoy. The handsome military bearing of the general, and the sweeping background landscape, relate to portraits by Reynolds and Raeburn, which Goya may have known through prints.

María Tomasa de Palafox, Marchioness of Villafranca

(Cat. 2448), Oil on canvas, 195 x 126 cm

She was born in 1780, a daughter of the countess of Montijo, and married Francisco de Borja Álvarez de Toledo y Gonzaga, who upon the death of his brother, the eleventh marquis of Villafranca, came into the family title and joined it to that of Medina-Sidonia. María Tomasa, who came from an art-loving and cultured family, was herself an amateur painter and became an honorary member of the Academy of San Fernando. In this portrait, signed "Goya 1805" and exhibited at the Academy later in that year, she is shown painting her husband.

The Countess of Chinchón (Cat. 7767)
Oil on canvas, 226 x 144 cm

María Teresa de Borbón y Vallabriga, a daughter of Charles III's brother Luis de Borbón and an Aragonese lady of the lower nobility, satisfied the wishes of the King Charles IV and Queen María Luisa by marrying the almighty minister Godoy, who was rumoured to be the Queen's paramour. As a result she and her siblings were given the family name of Borbón, forfeited when Luis was forced by Charles III to marry below his rank. In the correspondence between Queen María Luisa and Godoy, this portrait is reported to be in progress in April 1800. The Countess was pregnant with her first child, Carlota, who was born in October, and her condition is signaled by the ears of wheat in her headdress, a symbol of fertility. Goya, while capturing the aristocratic bearing and exalted position of María Teresa, has placed her in an indeterminate setting, dense with shadows that serve as a foil to her luminous, quasi-transparent figure, emphasizing her delicate and fragile appearance. Her folded hands and bashful smile contribute to her helpless, childlike air. The composition, which shortly antedates that of the grand *Family of Charles IV,* is masterly balanced through a carefully worked-out geometrical scheme. In many areas the flowing and precise brushwork leaves uncovered the pinkish underpainting, which Goya skilfully blends with his restricted range of colour.

Marchioness of Santa Cruz (Cat. 7070)
Oil on canvas, 124 x 207 cm

Born in 1784, a daughter of the duke and duchess of Osuna, and made marchioness of Santa Cruz by her marriage to José Gabriel de Silva y Waldstein in 1801, she was one of the most admired women of her time on account of her beauty and culture, a friend of poets and men of letters; Goya had portrayed her as a child with her family (Cat. 739).

Here she appears crowned with grapevine, her left arm resting on a lyre-shaped guitar that alludes to the classical god Apollo; thus Goya signals her fondness of poetry and her patronage of contemporary poets, presenting her, in the neoclassical vocabulary of the time, as a modern Erato, the muse of lyric poetry. By its excellent condition, this picture is exceptional in maintaining its original appearance, with tonal harmonies of a dazzling perfection.

Juana Galarza de Goicoechea (Cat. 4194)
Oil on copper, 8 cm Ø
Manuela Goicoechea y Galarza
(Cat. 7461)
Oil on copper, 8 cm Ø

On the occasion of his son Javier's marriage to Gumersinda Goicoechea in 1805, Goya painted six delightful miniature portraits of the bride's family: her father Miguel Martín de Goicoechea and her mother Juana Galarza, wealthy and liberal Madrid merchants who were the owners of a flourishing business of textiles and lace, and their four daughters. The Prado houses those of the mother and the eldest daughter, Manuela.

The Actor Isidoro Máiquez (Cat. 734)
Oil on canvas, 72 x 59 cm

Born in Cartagena in 1768, of actor parents, Máiquez studied in Paris under Talma and imported into Spain his new and forceful acting style. This portrait, signed "MAYQUEZ/POR GOYA/1807", is dated the year before the Peninsular War, and in it Goya's dramatic technique amazingly anticipates the future, even though it was probably calculated to meet such a specific condition as that of ensuring visibility from a distance without thereby lessening the force of the image.

General José Palafox on Horseback (Cat. 725)
Oil on canvas, 248 x 224 cm

Born in Saragossa in 1775 and a popular hero in the Peninsular War, Palafox was appointed captain-general of Saragossa in 1808. His skill as a politician and his gallantry as a soldier earned him the favour of both the Cortes and the people. He turned his home city into a symbol of patriotic resistance against the invaders, even at the cost of countless lives. This portrait, inscribed "EL EXCMO. SR.

D. JOSÉ PALAFOX Y MELCI, POR GOYA, AÑO DE 1814", was one that the painter felt especially satisfied with. It shows the horse rushing ahead, and the general, who wears in his hat the badge of the defenders of Saragossa, raising his sword as a signal to attack. The dark hues of the broad and bare landscape enhance the glowing image of the hero in a brightly lit foreground.

Self-Portrait (Cat. 723)
Oil on canvas, 46 x 35 cm

Signed "FR. GOYA PINTOR [?] ARAGONÉS /POR EL MISMO/1815". This outstandingly individual and intimate likeness was perhaps painted by the artist for his own home and the people nearest to him in the grim aftermath of the war against Napoleon, while political persecution under Ferdinand VII grew steadily worse. Goya was soon to withdraw from public life and isolate himself within the circle of his family and his closest friends.

An Unknown Woman (Josefa Bayeu?) (Cat. 722)
Oil on canvas, 82 x 58 cm

Tradition has it that this is a portrait of Josefa Bayeu, Goya's wife. However, the date of execution, which judging from the style of clothing must be later than 1800, is not consistent with the age of the purported sitter, since Josefa Bayeu died at sixty-five in 1812.

Manuela Téllez-Girón y Pimentel, Duchess of Abrantes (Cat. 7713)
Oil on canvas, 92 x 70 cm

The sitter was a daughter of the ninth duke of Osuna, born in 1793 and married to Ángel María de Carvajal, the eighth duke of Abrantes. She received a modern education and was fond of the arts and letters. Her grand-father the duke of Huesca inspired her with a passion for music, and it was as a singer that Goya portrayed her in this canvas, a commission from the duchess of Osuna in 1816. Inscribed "DOÑA MANUELA GIRÓN Y PIMENTEL. DUQ.SA DE ABRANTES. PR GOYA/ 1816", this is his last great likeness of a highborn lady.

Juan Bautista Muguiro (Cat. 2898)
Oil on canvas, 103 x 85 cm

Goya died in April 1828, and this is possibly his last known painting. The inscription mentioning his age, ("D.N JUAN DE MUGUIRO, POR/SU AMIGO GOYA, Á LOS/81 AÑOS, EN BURDEOS,/MAYO DE 1827"), is an old man's proud assertion of his ability to rise above his infirmities; but it also carries a hint that he was not fit to paint much else in what was to prove the last year of his life. Contemporary references indicate that his failing eyesight compelled him to paint with a magnifying glass, and that he concentrated more on his drawings, lithographs and miniature paintings on ivory than on the larger canvases, which required more effort. The sure touch of his brush, which lasted him from youth to early old age, has now turned shaky or wavering.

But that which in others might be a fault is here transformed, by the pictorial intelligence of the old master and his time-tried skill, into an abstract sublimation of matter, which is suggested with next to no support. Their sparkling, intangible colour suffices to recreate the papers and inkstand; for the wooden back of the chair or the yellow upholstery of its seat, Goya is satisfied with a few dashing strokes of his brush, without attempting to define form or material in the traditional way.

WALL PAINTINGS FROM THE *QUINTA DEL SORDO* *BLACK PAINTINGS* (1820-1823)

The paintings that decorated the house bought in 1819 by Goya in the outskirts of Madrid, referred to as the *Quinta del Sordo* ("House of the Deaf Man") before that date, have become popularly known by the name of *Black Paintings* on account of the dark and black pigments used in them, and also because of their grim subject matter: witches and their sabbaths, the violence of Saturn devouring his children or of Judith beheading Holofernes.

Photographs taken in the nineteenth century show that Goya's new house was two-storied and quite commodious, and those characteristics must have been crucial for his decision to decorate it in his own way, using a technique such as mural painting, which he had mastered to perfection and which made it possible for him to cover large wall expanses without too much exertion.

The painted decoration of the *Quinta* must have been executed between 1820, when Goya moved in, and 1823, when he left for Bordeaux. In 1828 his friend the painter Antonio Brugada, in whose arms Goya was later to die, made a full inventory of the house, including the *Black Paintings*.

These were distributed in two rooms, one on the ground floor and the other, of similar size, upstairs; Brugada gave them titles that perhaps reflected the ideas of Goya himself.

The *Black Paintings* remained in the *Quinta*, which the painter's grandson Mariano sold in 1859, until 1874. In 1873 the estate was acquired by Baron Émile d'Erlanger, who, being interested only in the paintings, had them removed by the painter and restorer Salvador Martínez Cubells. The baron tried to sell them in Paris in 1878, with no success, and finally donated them to the Spanish state in 1883, whereupon they were assigned to the Prado Museum.

Their condition is less than satisfactory. The intervention of Martínez Cubells, although it may have saved them from destruction, probably did serious damage, since X-rays show extensive areas where the original colour was lost. They also reveal overpainting, retouching and modifications that intensify the sombre and dark mood of the scenes, more to the aesthetic taste of 1870, the date when they were restored, than to that of the period when Goya painted them.

The *Black Paintings* have been crucial to the assessment of Goya's art in the modern world. The German expressionists, the surrealists and the representatives of other contemporary art movements, as well as writers and even film-makers, have pointed to this series of compositions by the elderly Goya, who was by then cut off from the surrounding world and creating with absolute freedom, as the germ of modern art. In spite of the myriad explanations offered by art and literary historians, writers, and even psychologists, these works remain elusive and puzzling, not only because of the difficulty of unraveling their contents, but also on account of their staggering formal break with the art of their time and their thrust into the future; yet it is a fact that they display many of the aesthetic problems, moral concerns and sense of humour that had characterized Goya's art since his youth. Connections may be discovered even with some drawings in his early Italian Sketchbook or, somewhat later, with the figures in early tapestry cartoons such as *The Blind Guitarist.*

Goya used the world of sorcery to denounce the depravity of human beings, whose very features are altered and whose faces become beastly masks in the most perverse of the "witches", whilst the superstition and ignorance of the masses materialize in pilgrimages and processions where individuals dress in the old-fashioned costumes of the seventeenth century. War and the political events of the day also have a place, along with fratricidal and pointless violence, so that these works never stray very far from the guidelines of morality and the rule of reason and progress which Goya advocated in his art throughout his life.

Other Paintings by Goya not in the Prado Museum

Amsterdam, Rijksmuseum: *Ramón Satué* (1823).
Besançon, Musée: *Cannibals.*
Bilbao, Museo de Bellas Artes: *Leandro Fernández de Moratín* (ca. 1810).
Budapest, Fine Arts Museum: *The Knifegrinder* and *The Water Carrier* (ca. 1810).
Cádiz, Oratorio de la Santa Cueva: *The Multiplication of Loaves and Fishes, The Last Supper* and *The Parable of the Wedding Garment* (1796-1797).
Cudillero (Asturias), Fundación Selgas-Fagalde: *Hannibal Looking on Italy from the Alps* (1772).
Chicago, Art Institute: *The Story of the Bandit Maragato* (1806-1807).
Dallas, Meadows Museum: *The Madhouse* (1794).
London, National Gallery: *The Picnic* (1788; sketch), *Witchcraft Scene* (1798), *Andrés del Peral* (ca. 1797).
London, Wellington Museum: *Wellington on Horseback* (1812).
Los Angeles, Norton Simon Museum: *Saint Jerome.*
Madrid, Academy of San Fernando: *Self-Portrait at the Easel* (ca. 1790), *La Tirana, Manuel Godoy, Juan de Villanueva* (1800-1805), *Ferdinand VII on Horseback* (1808), *An Inquisition Scene* (ca. 1810), *A Procession* (ca. 1810), *A Bullfight in a Village* (ca. 1810), *A Madhouse Scene* (ca. 1810).
Madrid, Banco de España: *The Count of Floridablanca* (ca. 1783), *The Count of Altamira* (1787), *The Marquis of Tolosa* (1787), *Francisco Javier de Larrumbe* (1787), *The Count of Cabarrús* (1788).
Madrid, Casa Ducal de Alba: *The Duchess of Alba in White* (1795).
Madrid, Museo Lázaro Galdiano: *The Witches' Sabbath, The Evil Spell* (1798), *The Harvest* (sketch), *The Entombment of Christ* (ca. 1780).
Madrid, Museo Municipal: *Allegory of the City of Madrid* (1810).
Madrid, Convento de los Padres Escolapios: *The Last Communion of Saint Joseph of Calasanz* (1819).

Madrid, Museo Romántico: *Saint Gregory the Great* (1796-1798).

Madrid, Museo Thyssen-Bornemisza: *Asensio Juliá* (ca. 1798).

Madrid, Palacio Real: *King Charles IV, Queen María Luisa.*

Madrid, Palacio de la Zarzuela: *Making Bullets* (ca. 1810), *Making Gunpowder* (ca. 1810).

Madrid, San Antonio de la Florida: Frescoes with a miracle of Saint Anthony of Padua (1798).

Madrid, San Francisco el Grande: *Saint Bernardino of Siena Preaching* (1782-1783).

Madrid, Private collections: *The Countess-Duchess of Benavente* (1785), *Ceán Bermúdez* (1798), *La Tirana, The Count and Countess of Fernán-Núñez* (1803), *Martín Miguel de Goicoechea* and *Juana Galarza* (1810), *A Shipwreck* (1794), A Fire By Night (1794), a series of cabinet pictures, Collection Marqués de la Romana (1798-1800), *The Maja and the Celestina on the Balcony* (ca. 1812).

Málaga, Collection Marqués de Larios: *Mariano Goya* (1809).

Malibu (Los Angeles), Paul Getty Museum: *The Marchioness of Santiago* (1809).

Minneapolis, Institute of Art: *Self-Portrait with Doctor Arrieta* (1820).

New York, Metropolitan Museum of Art: *The Countess of Altamira and Her Son* (1787-1788), *Manuel Osorio y Zúñiga* (1788), *Tiburcio Pérez Cuervo* (1820).

New York, Frick Collection: *María Martínez de Puga* (1824).

New York, The Hispanic Society of America: *The Duchess of Alba in Black.*

New York, Private collection: *Still Life with Dead Hares* (ca. 1800).

Pamplona, Museo de Bellas Artes, Diputación Foral: *The Marquis of San Adrián* (1804).

Paris, Musée du Louvre: *The Marchioness of La Solana* (ca. 1795), *Ferdinand Guillemardet* (1798).

Paris, Private collection: Portraits of Javier Goya in Grey and of His Wife (1806).

Reggio Emilia, Fondazione Magnani Rocca: *The Family of the Infante Don Luis* (1783).

Rome, private collection: *Portraits of Joaquín María Ferrer and of His Wife* (1824).
Seville, Cathedral: *Saints Justa and Rufina* (1814).
Seville, private collection: *The Annunciation* (1785).
Stockholm, Nationalmuseum: *Allegory of Time, Truth and History* (ca. 1798).
Switzerland, private collection: *Majas on the Balcony* (ca. 1812).
Toledo, Cathedral, Sacristy: *The Taking of Christ* (1798).
Valencia, Cathedral: *Saint Francis Borgia and a Possessed Man, Saint Francis Borgia Taking Leave of His Family (1788).*
Valencia, Museo de San Pío V: *Joaquina Candado.*
Valladolid, Convento de Santa Ana: *The Death of Saint Joseph, Saint Lutgard, Saints Bernard and Robert* (1787).
Washington, *The Marchioness of Pontejos* (ca. 1786), *Portraits of Bartolomé Sureda and of His Wife* (ca. 1804-1806), *Francisca Sabasa y García* (ca. 1804-1808), *The Book-seller's Wife* (ca. 1808).
Zaragoza, Museo de Bellas Artes: *Our Lady of the Pillar, The Death of Saint Francis Xavier* (ca. 1772).
Zaragoza, Basílica del Pilar: Frescoes in the "Coreto", *The Adoration of the Name of God* (1775); Cupola, *The Queen of Martyrs* (1780).
Zaragoza, Cartuja de Aula Dei: Frescoes with the Life of the Virgin Mary (1774).
Zaragoza, Ibercaja: *Self-Portrait* (1778).

Chronology

1746: Goya is born on March 30 in Fuendetodos (Saragossa).
1759: Studies painting and drawing in Saragossa, in the workshop of José Luzán.
1763: First trip to Madrid.
1766: Second trip to Madrid.
1771: Travels in Italy, with a lengthy stay in Rome. He also visits Venice, Parma, Genoa and other cities. Enters competition at the Academy of Parma.
1773: Marries Josefa Bayeu, sister of Francisco and Ramón.
1774: Frescoes in the Charterhouse of Aula Dei in Saragossa.
1775: Fresco on a vault of the Basílica del Pilar in Saragossa.
1776: First commissions of tapestry cartoons for the king, a kind of work he will paint until 1792.
1780: Elected academician of merit to the Royal Academy of Fine Arts of San Fernando.
1783: Works for the Infante don Luis de Borbón, brother of the king.
1785: Appointed assistant director of painting at the Academy.
1786: Appointed King's Painter. Birth of Javier, the only son that will survive him.
1790: Last series of tapestries for the royal palaces.
1792: Visits Cádiz and Seville, where he is taken seriously ill.
1793: Convalesces in Andalusia but is left deaf. Returns to Madrid in the summer.
1794: Presents to the Academy twelve cabinet pictures that mark the beginning of his independent production.
1795: Appointed director of painting at the Academy.
1796: Stays in Seville with Ceán Bermúdez. Relationship with the duchess of Alba begun in Sanlúcar de Barrameda.
1797: Second stay with the duchess of Alba in Sanlúcar. Resigns his directorship of painting at the Academy.
1798: Frescoes in the hermitage of San Antonio de la Florida.
1799: Etchings series, *Los Caprichos.* Appointed First King's Painter.
1804: Gregorio Ferro, a thoroughly neoclassical painter, obtains general directorship of the Academy against Goya.

1805: Javier Goya marries. Goya meets Leocadia Zorrilla.
1806: Birth of his grandson Mariano.
1808: Goya, an official at court, takes an oath of loyalty to king José Bonaparte.
1810: Makes his will with his wife Josefa Bayeu.
1811: José Bonaparte awards him the Royal Order of Spain.
1812: Death of Josefa Bayeu.
1814: Is cleared of charges of collaborating with the government of José Bonaparte. Attends a solemn session of the Academy presided by Ferdinand VII.
1816: Etchings series, *La Tauromaquia.* Beging *Los Disparates.*
1819: Tries lithography, a new technique. Falls gravely ill. Buys the "Quinta del Sordo", an estate outside Madrid. Lives with Leocadia Zorrilla and her daughter Rosarito, possibly his as well.
1820: Attends his last session at the Academy. Swears loyalty to the king and the Constitution.
1824: Asks leave from the king to take a water cure at Plombières in France. Goes to Paris in June, and to Bordeaux in September; Leocadia and Rosarito join him.
1825: Is extremely ill. Lithographs, *The Bulls of Bordeaux.* Miniatures on ivory.
1826: In Madrid, petitions the king for retirement; is granted a pension of 50,000 *reales.*
1827: Again in Madrid; returns to Bordeaux in September.
1828: Dies in Bordeaux on April 16, in his last home, rue Fossés-de-l'Intendance.

Selected Bibliography

Águeda, M.: "Los retratos ecuestres de Goya", in *Goya. Nuevas visiones. Homenaje a Enrique Lafuente Ferrari,* Madrid, 1987, pp. 39-59.

Andioc, R.: "En torno a los cuadros del Dos de Mayo en Goya", Osnabrück University, 1991.

Angulo Íñiguez, D.: "El *Saturno* y las *Pinturas Negras* de Goya", *Archivo Español de Arte,* 1962, pp. 173-177.

Arnaiz, J. M.: *Francisco de Goya. Cartones y tapices,* Madrid, 1987.

Beroqui, P.: "Una biografía de Goya escrita por su hijo", *Archivo Español de Arte,* 1927, pp. 99-100.

Beruete, A. de: *Goya, pintor de retratos,* Madrid, 1916.

Beruete, A. de: *Goya, composiciones y figuras,* Madrid, 1917.

Bozal, V.: *Imagen de Goya,* Madrid, Lumen, 1983.

Calvo Serraller, F. y otros: *Goya. La imagen de la mujer,* Madrid, Fundación Amigos del Museo del Prado, 2001 (ed. ing., Washington, 2002).

Camón Aznar, J.: *Francisco de Goya,* 4 vols., Zaragoza, 1980-82.

Cruzada Villaamil, G.: *Los tapices de Goya,* Madrid, 1870.

Gállego, J.: *Las "Majas" de Goya,* Madrid, 1982.

Garrido, C.: "Algunas consideraciones sobre la técnica de las *Pinturas Negras* de Goya", *Boletín del Museo del Prado,* 1984, pp. 4-40.

Gassier, P., and **Wilson, J.:** *Vie et Oeuvre de Francisco de Goya,* Freiburg, 1970.

Glendinning, N.: *The Interpretation of Goya's Black Paintings,* London, 1977.

Gudiol, J.: *Goya 1746-1828: Biografía, estudio analítico y catálogo de sus pinturas,* 4 vols., Barcelona, 1970.

Held, J.: *Die Genrebilder der Madrider Teppichmanufaktur und die Anfänge Goyas,* Berlin, 1971.

Helman, E.: *Trasmundo de Goya,* Madrid, 1983.

Lafuente Ferrari, E.: *Antecedentes, coincidencias e influencias del arte de Goya,* Madrid, 1947 (ed. 1987).

Licht, F.: *Goya. The Origins of Modern Temper in Art,* London, 1979.

Luna, J., and **Moreno, M.:** *Goya. 250 Aniversario,* Madrid, Museo del Prado, 1996.

Mena, M., and **Urrea, J.:** *El Cuaderno italiano de Goya,* Madrid, Museo del Prado, 1994.

Muller, P.: *Goya's Black Paintings. Truth and Reason in Light and Liberty,* New York, 1984.
Pérez Sánchez, A. E.: "Goya en el Prado. Historia de una colección singular", in *Goya. Nuevas visiones. Homenaje a Enrique Lafuente Ferrari,* Madrid, 1987, pp. 307-22.
Pita Andrade, J. M.: "Observaciones en torno a los cartones para tapices", *Goya,* 1979, pp. 232-59.
Pita Andrade, J. M.: *Goya. Obra, vida y sueños,* Madrid, 1989.
Rose, I.: *Manuel Godoy, patrón de las artes y coleccionista,* 2 vols., Madrid, 1983.
Salas, X. de: "Un boceto de Goya para la Inmaculada del Colegio de Calatrava", *Archivo Español de Arte,* 1977, pp. 1-8.
Salas, X. de: "Minucias sobre Goya. Sobre el signifiado de las Pinturas Negras de la Quinta", *Estudios sobre literatura y arte dedicados al Prof. Emilio Orozco Díaz,* Granada, 1979, pp. 245-58.
Salas, X. de: *Goya en Madrid,* Madrid, 1979.
Sambricio, V. de: *Tapices de Goya,* Madrid, 1946.
Sánchez Cantón, F. J.: "Goya, pintor religioso", *Revista de Ideas Estéticas,* 1946, pp. 277-310.
Sánchez Cantón, F. J.: *Vida y obras de Goya,* Madrid, 1951.
Sánchez Cantón, F. J.: *Goya y sus Pinturas Negras de la Quinta del Sordo,* Madrid, 1963.
Tomlinson, J.: *Goya. The Tapestry Cartoons and Early Career at the Court of Madrid,* New York, 1989.
Torrecillas, C.: "Nueva documentación fotográfica sobre las pinturas de la Quinta del Sordo de Goya", *Boletín del Museo del Prado,* 1985, pp. 87-99.
Vega, J., Glendinning, N., and **Portús, J.:** *Estudiar a los maestros Velázquez y Goya,* Zaragoza, 2000.
Viñaza, Conde de la: *Goya. Su tiempo, su vida, sus obras,* Madrid, 1887.
VV.AA.: *Goya,* Madrid, 2002.
Wilson-Bareau, J.: *Goya. El Capricho y la Invención. Cuadros de gabinete, bocetos y miniaturas,* Madrid, Museo del Prado, 1993 (Eng. ed. 1994).
Yriarte, C.: *Goya. Sa biographie, les fresques, les toiles, les tapisseries, les eaux-fortes et le catalogue de l'oeuvre,* Paris, 1867.

Museo Nacional del Prado
General Information

Villanueva Building
Paseo del Prado, s/n. 28014 Madrid
Tel.: 91 330 28 00 / 91 330 29 00 Fax: 91 330 28 56
E-mail: museo.nacional@museodelprado.es
Website: www.museoprado.es
Wheelchair access available.

Museum hours
Tuesday to Sunday and public holidays: 9:00 a.m. to 8:00 p.m.
December 24 and 31 and January 6: 9:00 a.m. to 2:00 pm.
Last entry 30 minutes before closing.
Visitors are requested to start vacating galleries 10 minutes before closing.
Closed on Mondays, 1 January, Good Friday, 1 May and 25 December.
Note: Please consult possible changes in opening hours and other services in the Museum.

Admission Charges
Permanent collection: 6 €
Reduced admission fee: 3 €

- EU citizens members of large families
- Students under 25 from non-EU countries
- Youth card holders
- Cultural and educational groups (by prior arrangement)

Free Admission (with ID):

- Visitors under 18.
- EU citizens over 65, pensioners, unemployed, registered disabled.
- EU students under 25.
- Professors/teachers in areas related to the Museum collections.
- National and local tour guides
- Fundación Amigos del Museo del Prado.
- Members of national or international museum associations.

Free Admission for all visitors:

- Tuesday to Saturday: 6:00 p.m. to 8:00 p.m.
- Sunday: 5:00 p.m. to 8:00 p.m.
- May 2 and 18, October 12, December 6.

Temporary exhibitions and combined entrance fee (consult price).

Coffee Shop

Tuesday to Sunday and public holidays: 9:00 a.m. to 7:15 p.m.
December 24 and 31 and January 6: 9:00 a.m. to 1:20 p.m.

Restaurant

Tuesday to Sunday and public holidays: 11:30 a.m. to 4:00 p.m.

Shops

Tuesday to Sunday and public holidays: 9:00 a.m. to 7:45 p.m.
December 24 and 31 and January 6: 9:30 a.m. to 1:30 p.m.

Public Transport

Metro: Banco de España and Atocha
Bus: 9, 10, 14, 19, 27, 37 and 45
Train: Atocha Station
From Airport: Airport Metro.

Fundación Amigos del Museo de Prado General Information

Museo del Prado
Ruiz de Alarcón, 21, ground floor.
28014 Madrid
Tel: 91 420 20 46
Fax: 91 429 50 20
E-mail: info@amigosmuseoprado.org
Website: www.amigosmuseoprado.org
Office tours: Monday to Friday: 9:30 a.m. to 2:30 p.m.